88 Keys To Unlocking The Enlightened Soul

Torrey James Lystra

88 Keys To Unlocking The Enlightened Soul
Published in 2017 by Red Hawk Books
Copyright c 2017 by Torrey James Lystra
All rights reserved
Printed in USA

Cover Painting entitled; "Unlocking The Enlightened Soul" by Torrey James Lystra

Special thanks to Catherine TerBurgh and Carol Lystra regarding their editing assistance

The Library of Congress has catalogued this edition as follows:
The Library of Congress Control Number: 2017937765
Red Hawk Books, Gig Harbor, WA
Lystra, Torrey James, 1952
88 Keys To Unlocking The Enlightened Soul
ISBN: 0989285146
ISBN 13: 9780989285148
Red Hawk Books, Gig Harbor, Washington
PBK.

TABLE OF CONTENTS

INTRODUCTION

"88 Keys To Unlocking The Enlightened Soul" is the third book in my "Sacred Earth" series. This volume addresses a diverse spectrum of subjects regarding the sevenfold nature of being human, fire, supernatural talent, life, death, the human soul, spiritual enlightenment, karma, cause and effect, angels, Great Spirit, sacred technology, astral travel, life force, and so much more.

The knowledge revealed within is organized for easy access to review or ponder that which you have an interest. These "88 Keys" were born from the mystical, meditative, and spiritual questions asked of me while carrying out my work as a healer and seer described "In The Spirit of Black Elk: Preserving a Sacred Way" and "An Angel and a Shaman." In those true stories about how my life merged with an ancient lineage of powerful humble shamans I share some of the phenomena I experienced including the restoration of sight to the blind eye of one of my own sons. Mystery, sweat, intent, fate, karma, past lives, soul, focus, study, practice, commitment, curiosity, natural law, courage, prayer, fasting, love, and more may be found within "88 Keys To Unlocking The Enlightened Soul."

May you discover the Light that you seek through the harmony of the "notes" represented in these "88 Keys." They are meant to be "played" as often as you wish so that you might reach even greater heights and understanding. Before you begin your journey within this new volume, I would like to pass along to you some advice given to me by the celestial being that I first met within the Kings Chamber of the Great Pyramid during my initiation ceremony into these ancient mysteries back in January 1990. These were her words to me then that I have attempted to live by:

In order for you to be happy you must first consciously choose the outcome of happiness above all the other choices that will be available to you while you occupy the body you currently reside in. Try to be compassionate and caring towards others. Kindness is a proper response to almost every action while you are on Earth. Try to be in service to humanity in some manner. Not only will you be a positive influence on the society you are a part of, but those in service to mankind are usually moving towards the activation of the supernatural talents that exist potentially within every human soul. If you acquire important knowledge or wisdom on your journey, please share it without your primary concern being financial compensation. This refreshing attitude will still be rewarded in an appropriate manner, and you may avoid a pathway related to greed and avarice which is wrought with peril. Rejoice and be grateful for your life. To live a life filled with joy allows you to walk in gratitude for all the blessings you have received and it is with gratitude that you are able to communicate with Great Spirit in a direct manner. Express what you love, not what you hate. Haters are usually shallow, selfish, angry, and violent beings, while those who know and express love possess the highest most wondrous aspect of being human. Respect all beings, not just the human variety. Some people are too arrogant to respect all life and fall short of the highest benefits of this worthy virtue. Do not get too high or too low with your successes or failures, as they are simply experiences you have chosen to learn from. Take care of your body as you may need it to accomplish all that you came here for. If you occupy a body that is in ill health, try to learn from that experience that you more than likely chose for yourself either between lives or unknowingly via the universal law of cause and effect in this cycle of living. Be willing to acknowledge new ideas. Think through and examine all opinions. Do not hurry through your life, savor it like fine wine and be free.

May the words that I share be like a gentle wind moving sweetly through your immortal soul.

DEDICATION

This writing is dedicated to my mother who was a beautiful human being both inside and out. She was the glue that held our family together and her care for each of us was splendid in numerous ways. I have especially fond memories of our early years together when she served as my personal teacher, elementary school room mother, Cub Scout leader, nurturer, confidant, and advisor. Mom often had a pot of coffee brewing for she and a visiting friend that needed her help in some way. She was a deeply spiritual and giving human being who graced the world with her smile. The "88 Keys" which play a part in the title of this book, are also the number of keys on a piano which served her as a gifted musician, singer, and choir director. Even as a victim of Alzheimer's disease during the last 12 years of her life, she was an inspiration to all who knew her.

QUESTION 1

Q You mentioned in our ceremony tonight the sevenfold nature of every human being and how you felt knowledge of these principles could act as a compass for our lives. Could you review that concept for us now to help us understand precisely what you meant?

TJL There are many different versions of this wisdom that show up in some of the ancient texts that have survived the geological events at the end of each of the worlds that have preceded our own, however, this teaching from my angel is the most complete of the many that only partially cover this topic.

The first of these principles is our physical body. This is the least important of these seven aspects of humankind and yet we must each master the care and attention of our bodies since they house the living Spirit that resides within us.

The second of these principles is our astral body. This body appears similar to the physical body yet is composed of a finer matter that remains invisibly connected to our physical body by a thread of light to its ethereal form on the astral plane.

The third of these principles is our vital force which I refer to as prana. This is universal energy and essential to our lives. It is found in all things having life, in every atom, and is everywhere. We utilize it in its material manifestation yet it is not matter.

The next four principles go to make up the thinking part of a human being and are considered higher than the first three. They function on three separate planes that at times blend imperceptibly with each other as we advance in the unfoldment of our soul. They comprise our intelligence.

The fourth of these principles is our instinctive or animal mind. The instinctive mind is responsible for passions, desires, instincts, and brute emotions. We will discard this principle at the moment of our death along with the previously mentioned three. Many human beings have not yet advanced beyond this aspect in their soul unfoldment.

The fifth principle, and the first of the next three aspects of mind that are infinite and become a permanent part of our soul, lifetime after lifetime, is self-consciousness or intellect. This principle allows us to sense our first conception of the "I" that is who we really are, and we begin to think for ourselves, analyze, and draw conclusions.

The sixth principle is our spiritual mind. This aspect directly aids us in the growth and maturity of our soul and is where inspiration and all that we consider good, noble, and great reside.

The seventh principle is Spirit. I call this our Divine Spark. Masters refer to this principle as the soul within the soul and words do not really do it justice. It is that something within us that I call the sacred flame of Great Spirit.

QUESTION 2

Q What would your broad definition of a shaman include?

TJL My definition of a shaman would include healer, seer, mystic, poet, artist, philosopher, prophet, advisor, spirit talker, astral traveler, weather manipulator, culture bearer, clairvoyant, drummer, singer, teacher, and person able to assume other forms.

QUESTION 3

Q You mentioned in our ceremony that fire had special meaning to you. Could you please clarify your relationship to fire?

TJL Yes, it is frequently thought by those unfamiliar with the highest aspects of a humble shaman's work that we worship fire. That is not the case at all. However, I do have a deep respect for it. There have also been moments when I have experienced an overwhelming awareness of the power of it. In my beginning work with Grandfather

Wallace Black Elk, as his fire keeper, I learned to honor it, to work with it closely, and to listen for its messages. During my own stone-people-lodge ceremonies, the tremendous heat it generated in the stones caused me to humble myself before it. I learned that each part of a fire is significant. A fire's sparks represent love. A fire's embers represent soul. A fire's flames represent our material world. Most important of all, a fire's smoke represents a pathway to Great Spirit. Grandfather sometimes referred to Great Spirit as the "Fire of Life" and he described that aspect as the intelligence that moves the universe. The one principle that underlies all phenomena in nature is fire.

QUESTION 4

Q What changes would you make to our civilization if you could wave a magic wand to improve things in an instant?

TJL I would change the relationship most people currently maintain with our planet from one of neglect and lack of regard, to one of love and caring. I would create more efficient shelters so that everyone could have one. I would create more vibrant foods so that hunger could not exist. I would establish clean water everywhere along with effective sustainable water conservation measures so that all beings could have as much water as they required. I would simplify our needs and evolve more responsive communities that would eliminate all wasteful resource practices. Pollution would eventually be almost completely eliminated. Education would be encouraged for all people at no charge. Job creation would become the most prominent part of helping people feel right about their contribution to society. Every person that wanted a job could have one. I would utilize the internet and social media to bring the world together into a global community that worked to help each other. Doing purposeful physical harm to another human being would become an outrageous action and therefore war would become a distant memory. In the words of John Lennon, "Some people say that I am a dreamer, but I am not the only one!"

QUESTION 5

Q Could you share more information about the "supernatural talent" or "spiritual gifts" you have experienced in your work as a humble shaman?

TJL My Angel explained to me that what Grandfather Black Elk referred to as "supernatural talent" or "spiritual gift" to bring about what others might refer to as miracles, exists in an innate potential state within the soul of every human being. She went on to explain that in past ages religious and political hierarchies hid this knowledge from the masses because they feared mankind would misuse it. Those in power also hoped to maintain their positions of control over humanity while vast libraries describing this knowledge were burned to the ground and many ancient sources were destroyed. Calling these spiritual powers "super natural" is simply a way to identify them beyond what we would generally consider as natural. They are available to all who apply themselves to helping others, and have been hidden, misrepresented, mistranslated, manipulated, thought to be myth, and now days mostly forgotten. The avatar Jesus knew them to be very real when he stated, "As I do you can do also." At this time in our development awareness of the potential treasures of the human soul are vitally important for the evolution of all humankind.

The "supernatural talent" or "spiritual gift" is literally:

* certain knowledge about the eternal aspects of the soul of man

* the ability to read the mind of any being in any universe,
* the awareness of all past lifetimes,
* the ability of assuming any form in any universe,
* the ability to understand any sound in any universe.
* the insight into the nature of any object in any universe.

Only a being who achieves perfect enlightenment will acquire them all.

QUESTION 6

Q Could you explain how angels fit into our material world?

TJL As you know from my writing and the sacred ceremonies you have participated in I first met my angel during my initiation ceremony within the Kings Chamber of the Great Pyramid in Egypt back in January, 1990. I often refer to her as my spiritual guide and my experience over my years of working with her is that she is a wise and loving being. She explained to me that angels are known to pull back the curtain on the spiritual realms for human beings. She informed me that most angels occupy a separate plane from our material world. She discussed with me that angels were given free will similar to human beings. She explained that it was her choice to serve humanity in our realm and that within that service she has found perfect freedom. She stated that angels are able to assume ethereal bodies as needed to carry out a task and that some of the highest angels from her world were instrumental in our creation on this material plane.

QUESTION 7

Q I have never heard you utter any words to the effect that we should all follow in your foot steps and do things exactly as you have regarding your "Sacred Way." Why is that?

TJL I truly care about each of you and I expect you to utilize your own hearts and minds to decide what is best for you. I am not a great proponent of followers and believe all too often people find themselves giving away their personal power to someone else rather than continue with their own first hand inspiration from the Divine. I try to see the good and truth in other pathways of attainment and belief systems. Accept what appeals to you now, and as you progress revisit other pathways that may open up to you later. You are each unique so trust what feels right for you and do no harm to another being in the process.

QUESTION 8

Q Do you consider Buddhism another viable "Sacred Way?"

TJL Yes, Buddhism is actually called "the Way" by those who walk that path because Buddha felt illumination could not be taught. He understood "the Way" as a vehicle that might lead his followers beyond concepts and thoughts where the knowledge of silence became the experience of sacred wisdom.

QUESTION 9

Q You mentioned in our stone-people-lodge ceremony this evening that you personally admired the ways of a Bodhisattva and that if you had not discovered the "Sacred Way" you practice that it may have been a path that you sought. Can you explain what a Bodhisattva is and why you feel such a strong connection?

TJL A Bodhisattva represents illumination in Buddhism and it was said about them that they had the ability to "awaken humanity" in our world.

Legends state that after the first of these beings was about to achieve complete release from having to come back into another body after reincarnation he heard the rocks, the trees, and all of creation lamenting the fact he would be leaving. In his selfless, boundless compassion he renounced his release from which he had striven many lifetimes to accomplish, and chose to continue to serve as a teacher in our world to help other beings.

QUESTION 10

Q "In the Spirit of Black Elk: Preserving a Sacred Way" you shared a rather fascinating chapter on your flying like a Red Hawk, your Spirit given namesake. Would you care to help us understand what that chapter was about?

TJL Over my years of completing stone-people-lodge healing ceremonies there have been occasions when those within our circle noticed I had literally gone through a transformation into the form of a Red Hawk for a period of time within the space of that structure to travel to another realm to bring back information to this one. That writing is simply a re-creation of how it feels to fly like a Red Hawk during one of those experiences.

QUESTION 11

Q I would like to know what your position is on the traditional view of Heaven and Hell?

TJL Heaven and Hell are simply psychological states of mind, not physical locations. They were added to the consciousness of mankind by other human beings who hoped to control the masses by the belief in these places of punishment and reward. After death some people create their own versions of such states while working in the astral world between lives to satisfy their earthly belief.

They consider their creations within the astral world as physical locations. However, there is no place of eternal damnation and punishment nor heavenly abode and eternal reward. When the avatar Jesus spoke about the "kingdom of heaven" he was referring to a state of being that exists within the soul of every human. Historically, everything that exists above our Earth has commonly been referred to as "the heavens" and many times "the heavens" refers to other planes of existence above our own.

QUESTION 12

Q The older I get the more anxiety I feel about time passing. What do you suggest?

TJL If you are anxious about time passing, something important may be missing from your life. Look deeply at what that is and take action. When your life comes to fulfillment your anxiety will disappear. If it is death that you fear, knowledge and understanding the truth about the seven principles of being human will help you on your journey.

QUESTION 13

Q "In the Spirit of Black Elk: Preserving a Sacred Way" you explained that your Grandfather considered sacred technology as the knowledge, wisdom, rituals, and ceremonies humble shamans have utilized since the first age of the current version of mankind. Could you clarify that statement for us?

TJL Grandfather used to remind me, "Grandson, we can never duplicate the intelligence, energy, and power of Great Spirit, however, we are able to work within the laws of nature in accord with that power to create what many beings might consider miracles through these "Sacred Ways." From my perspective we enter into the wisdom of the universe via this ancient technology which begins by looking within and comes to fruition with the complete awareness of the treasures found within the human soul. Many of these practices date back to the earliest versions of humankind in our present form.

QUESTION 14

Q I am grateful for the opportunity you gave us this evening to experience a stone-people-lodge ceremony. You have reminded me that I have direct access to Great Spirit if I make the effort in a humble way. Your words and songs are resonating with me still. Do you have any further advice to give me before I leave this evening?

TJL My advice to you would be to enjoy your life, savor your happiness, cherish your sacred time,

work in service to others, walk in beauty and freedom, and do no harm to another.

QUESTION 15

Q Would you define karma for me?

TJL Karma is the science of effects produced by causes. It comes from the Sanskrit word "Kri," meaning to do or to act. It refers directly to the effect of all of your actions in life. Many people and religions are confused by the Law because they erroneously believe that punishment is central to how it works. Karma is simply that which comes from an action. It applies to stars, planets, suns, and nations, as well as human beings. If our actions set up a condition in our lives then events will appear as the effect of the cause put in motion. The avatar Jesus attempted to simplify the law by stating "As you sew, so shall you reap." He taught that we are each responsible for our lives. My angel explained that Jesus also shared that Karma is sometimes carried over to a person's next incarnation. She states that there is a plane of the Divine Mind where the causes we set in motion reside, before they materialize in our lives. A balancing of all causes occurs there.

QUESTION 16

Q Certain human beings tell us that they must have been exceptional people in their past lives because of the all of the personal wealth they have accumulated this lifetime. Do you have any comment on this sentiment?

TJL It is pure illusion to believe spiritual advancement leads directly to material wealth. Several religions preach that overwhelming material wealth will be yours if you follow their specific

doctrine in a specific fashion. Please do not be
fooled by such dogma.

QUESTION 17

Q Why do you use the words Great Spirit instead of God when describing divinity?

TJL I have seen all of the other words used to describe God lead to enormous divisions, chaos, and spread hatred among many peoples who love to argue over a silly name difference for this supreme aspect. I began to utilize the words Great Spirit after I met Grandfather and it seemed to sum up appropriately a truthful yet simple concept for that being. Great Spirit is not an old man with a beard riding a cloud. The God described in the Bible is sometimes unjust, vindictive, cruel, and at times a tyrant, none of which describe the Great Spirit I am familiar with. Great Spirit is the supreme all, the absolute essence of being and non-being, the light and life of the universe, and the invisible soul in Nature.

QUESTION 18

Q How would you define Nature?

TJL When I speak about Nature I am referring to the sum total of everything that is. Nature is a perpetual becoming. The chemical compounds are the same in a mountain as a wild flower. They are the same in a human being as in an insect. They are the same in an elk as in a cedar tree. When you refer to Nature you refer to the organic as well as the inorganic. It is all life and constantly changing.

QUESTION 19

Q You have shared with us the importance of the circle from your perspective within the stone-people-lodge ceremonies we have done together. Your Grandfather Wallace Black Elk's adopted Grandfather Nicholas Black Elk is known to have delivered a now famous speech many years ago on that topic. Could you provide us with his perspective and philosophy regarding a circle?

I keep a version of it that one of Grandfather's nephews gave me in my notebook. I will retrieve

it for you and read to you if you will allow me…
Back in 1863 Nicholas Black Elk stated these now
famous words, "Everything an Indian does is in
a circle. That is because the power of the world
always works in circles and everything tries to be
round. In the olden days all the power came from
the sacred hoop of the nation and so long as the
hoop was unbroken the people flourished. The
flowering tree was the center of the hoop and the
circle of the four quarters nourished it. The East
gave peace and light, the South warmth, the West
rain, and the North gave strength and endurance.
Everything the power of the Earth does is in a
circle. The sky is round and I have heard the Earth
is round like a ball, and so are the stars. The wind
in its great power whirls and birds make nests in
circles. The sun comes forth and goes down again
in a circle. The moon does the same and both are
round. Even the seasons form a great circle in their

changing and always come back again where they were. The life of a man is a circle. So it is with everything, where power moves."

QUESTION 20

Q You mentioned in our healing ceremony tonight that a humble shaman is sometimes required to leave his physical body to acquire information from other realms to help someone with a specific problem or sickness. Can you help me understand this action more precisely?

TJL The process that I was involved with during those moments is commonly referred to as astral travel. It is accomplished through the use of a person's astral body, a less dense replica of a person's physical body that resides on the astral plane. The astral plane is separated from our physical material plane, not by distance or direction. It is separated by a difference in the octave of vibration. In the physical plane we have only three dimensions; height, width, and breadth. No matter what direction we move in we are traveling in one of those ways. Wherever the material plane exists the astral plane exists also, separated only by curves, angles, and vibration. To move to the astral plane you have to focus your attention there. Thought is instantaneously creative there. What you are thinking becomes manifest instantly therefore it is imperative that you remain in control of your thoughts. In the material plane you think in terms of time, space, and distance. In the astral plane there is no distance, no direction, no up, no down, no North, no South, no East or no West. Outside of the material plane you are free of it. You are outside of time, and the dimensions of the material world. Limitation is in the material plane. Most of you have experienced astral travel while sleeping but as yet are not able to hold those memories.

QUESTION 21

Q It is my undetanding that you feel education is one of the most powerful ways to help other human beings progress in the growth and advancement of their souls. I am aware you have accomplished a great deal of teaching within the confines of your stone-people-lodge ceremonies and I wonder if you have done any other types of teaching this lifetime?

TJL In my career as a park ranger and supervising park ranger I gave hundreds of programs to improve what I perceived to be a flawed relation-ship that many people have with our planet. I worked with both children and adults to share my love and understanding of the natural world with them in my hope that it might help them interface with nature in an appropriate manner in their lives. Since moving to the Northwest my em-phasis shifted to mainstream education and why it seemed to be failing many young people. I have been an advocate for passing local education related bond issues and wage increases for teachers who I consider some of the most under-appreciated wage earners in our society. I decided I wanted to be on the front lines of their efforts locally and taught as a guest teacher at an overcrowded local High School when my schedule allowed for many years. I found it to be one of the most challenging jobs I have ever been a part of. I was forced to utilize all of my skills to manage a diverse range of learn-ing abilities and backgrounds. I found that many of those young adults had given up on learning at that level and those kids I attempted to encourage to at least find something they loved and learn more about that.

QUESTION 22

Q Could you share more about your fascination with the stars Sirius and Orion which you briefly mentioned in our ceremony tonight?

TJL There is a pattern of stars that shows up in relationship to ancient structures around our planet. It is the Orion nebulae. That nebula contains around three thousand stars in various forms. It is basically a stellar birthing center. The Orion constellation is one of the most prominent within it and was said to be linked with magical creation by the ancients. The Egyptians relate many stories of how their race descended from Orion. Osiris was said to have originated there and is considered one of the founding fathers of that race. The goddess Isis was said to have originated from the star Sirius. I devote a chapter to my fascination with this subject within my second book entitled "Meteor Shower."

Egyptian shamans believe that Osiris will return someday. They believe the Great Pyramid was built as a launching pad for a person's soul and that an intergalactic star gate exists within. Many ceremonial sites around the world contain alignments related to what we call the stars of Orion's belt. Teotihuacan near Mexico City, the Great Pyramids in Egypt, even the Hopi in America aligned cities to this design. Orion was very important to the ancients and remains so to this day. This region in our universe played a major role in the prehistory of humankind.

QUESTION 23

Q When I experienced your teaching and healing work in Japan you mentioned that the soil on
which your sacred pipe, medicine bag, and other
accoutrements resided upon was special to you in
some manner. I was one of the many people who
came to request your help during your stay in my
country. Would it be improper for me to ask you
about that soil now?

TJL Not at all, the soil was collected from mole
mounds which my Lakota teachers knew to be

extremely powerful. That soil is one aspect of the healing energies Grandfather shared with me. Prayer ties are usually tied and placed around my altar made up of this soil by the person who has asked for my assistance. I create a perimeter circle with the prayer ties and then create a rudimentary drawing of the person asking for the help in that soil. I have found it to be a helping factor on many occasions and I utilized it throughout most of the sacred pipe work that I completed in Japan.

QUESTION 24

Q Could you help me understand what you mean when you speak about prana?

TJL Prana is the essence of life and the vital force which animates matter. The earliest recorded history recognizing this energy appears in China where it was known as ch'i. It is referred to as prana in Indian yogic texts. In Japan it was known as k'i. This life force sustains us here on Earth and is considered universal energy. Though it is in all forms of matter it is not matter itself. I utilize it in several aspects of the sacred work that I am involved with. It has relieved pain in some of those that I have helped. It can be projected at a distance. It can be accumulated through the air you breathe, the food you eat, or the liquid you consume. Within a stone-people-lodge, I was able to see an indication of who people are as their prana fields glow in that environment. All living organisms exchange this energy with the universe. When the flow of this energy is restricted or becomes imbalanced then the organism becomes sick. If the flow ceases altogether, then so does that individual life.

QUESTION 25

Q You mentioned in our ceremony tonight that 7/23 is an important date for you. Could you explain the significance of that date?

TJL It is the date of our calendar year when the star Sirius dips below the horizon and comes up to rise before the sun to create the effect that we are living on a planet with two suns. It really is an extraordinary site that will remind you of a science fiction movie scenario if you are ever in a position to see it in person in the southern hemisphere of our planet.

QUESTION 26

Q You utilized a visual aid in your storytelling within the stone-people-lodge tonight, the "vesica pisces." You explained how you sometimes see two overlapping spheres, one natural and the other supernatural during a healing occurrence. Within that overlapping area is where you sometimes see those you are trying to help. I found it a fascinating way of sharing with us an important part of your process. I realize that form is prominent in geometry and wonder if the "vesica pisces" has any other historical context.

TJL The avatar Jesus is displayed within the vesica pisces in several European churches.

QUESTION 27

Q You mentioned your Grandfather felt a pure mind and heart were essential to carry on the work of a humble shaman. Could you explain how this purity helps you in your work?

TJL Kindness, compassion, and unselfishness, are outward signs of the pure heart and mind of the enlightened shaman. A shaman in this state is able to communicate with the intelligence of Great Spirit through different elements within Nature. We are able to discern the difference between malevolent energies and benevolent energies in all dimensions. We are able to literally construct our lives to be free to go where Spirit leads us. We have the ability to leave our physical bodies behind to explore other realms when that is called for in ceremony. We are able to listen to our spirit guides from other planes to understand how best to serve others with our work. We are able to at times ma-nipulate space and time.

QUESTION 28

Q Many ancient texts speak of "the four conditions of mankind." Are you familiar with this perspective and if so what are the conditions they refer to?

TJL What you speak to is the theory that human beings contain four frequencies originating and consisting of light. It postulates that everything we experience is found within those four realities. They are as follows: wakefulness, which includes all of our earth related experiences, dreamtime, which includes all of our out-of-body consciousness, dreamlessness, which refers to a state of being beyond dreams where no desires exists, and total bliss, which speaks to our oneness with Divinity.

QUESTION 29

Q Could you please help me understand what exactly time and space are from your perspective?

TJL Space is without dimension and is self-existent. Time is the illusion produced by the succession of our various states of consciousness divided mathematically into past, present, and future. They are relative terms belonging to the limited minds of man. The unlimited and most important definition of each term is eternity and infinity.

QUESTION 30

Q Could you define your use of the word fate for us within the context of your teaching tonight?

TJL It is the most likely effect of the cause that we have set in motion in our lives through the actions that we have taken. Just as light can be bent by mind, so also can fate be bent at times by a humble shaman with proper intent thereby allowing for a different outcome than might have originally been expected.

QUESTION 31

Q What do you mean when you speak about a spiral without end?

TJL Each human being's numerous lifetimes are represented by a spiral without end which I define as your "great life." This form is symbolic for the eternal aspect of your soul.

QUESTION 32

Q If I asked you what was the most important thing for human beings to pay attention too while we live our lives on this material plane, what would that be?

TJL The most important thing for any human being to pay attention to is the nurturing, growth, and advancement of the soul. Knowledge about the human soul and the power it confers on mankind is vitally important for our next evolutionary step towards the realization that we are really spiritual beings living in physical bodies each steadily advancing towards perfection through the unfoldment of our soul.

QUESTION 33

Q Could you please explain to me what you mean by "the enlightened state of a shaman."

TJL The "enlightened state of a shaman" refers to a condition free of illusion when a shaman's finite consciousness becomes one with the higher powers. It is made possible by the level of advancement of the soul. During this time any one of the "supernatural talents" available to the shaman may be manifested for the purpose of helping another being. This is a temporary sublime condition as opposed to the permanent nature of perfect enlightenment.

QUESTION 34

Q I have heard other people tell me that have been a part of your ceremonies that stones sometimes mysteriously appear out of thin air to become a part of a ceremony in some way. Would you mind commenting on these stones, and are you aware of a stone known to historians as Lapis exillis.

TJL Stones are perfect examples of a family from the mineral kingdom not yet fully understood by most human beings. However, in certain indigenous societies such as the Lakota shamans of my

Grandfather's lineage, this knowledge along with other remnants of ancient wisdom was preserved. Most human beings are not willing to believe that a rock can possess an intelligence that allows it to perform work that is beyond the intellect of man. Lapis exillis was a stone that many believe started the Holy Grail dialogue. It was said to have fallen from the heavens during the years when the Knights Templar had great prominence around our planet. It was rumored to contain powers over sickness and aging.

QUESTION 35

Q Could you clarify what you mentioned about inner rapture in your teaching this evening?

TJL Human beings are so engaged in our material world that many of them spend every waking moment trying to impress others with their personal wealth and outer lives. They forget the inner rapture and joy associated with simply being alive in a physical body and looking within to advance and grow their soul which is really why we are all here.

QUESTION 36

Q What has it meant for you to be a humble shaman this lifetime?

TJL It has given me a clear awareness of the true
art of living a life filled with Spirit and has provided
me an avenue to serve others in a humble manner.

QUESTION 37

Q Could you help us understand precisely why a stone-people-lodge ceremony might be beneficial to us?

TJL It is a ceremony designed to cleanse the doors of perception for each person in the circle to allow participants to view their lives in a clear manner. It is a time to quiet your mind and follow your heart. You will have an opportunity to ritually purify mind, body, and Spirit. You may perceive with a mythological sense of time and space. You may understand that anyone can communicate with Great Spirit. It may allow you a few moments to express your gratitude for your life and others. You may discover a literal opening to your "Sacred Way" within one of these ceremonies.

QUESTION 38

Q What is our soul's highest purpose here on Earth?

TJL Our soul's highest purpose is to grasp the reality of Great Spirit in all things which I refer to as enlightenment.

QUESTION 39

Q In your books you referenced the "Great Light Brother and Sisterhood" as those beings who have helped guide mankind since our creation. Are you able to share any further information about those beings at this time?

TJL Those perfected beings agreed to occupy bodies again, starting in an early cycle of humankind, to assist us on our quest to overcome matter and help with the evolution of every soul as we progress towards perfection. They have been referred to by many names such as initiates, adepts, magi, wise men, avatars, great souls, and simply the "brotherhood." Though many of them have remained hidden from the masses since our inception, and many of you will be skeptical with their mention, they are real beings and have been referred to on occasion throughout mainstream historical records and ancient texts.

QUESTION 40

Q Several religions maintain that human beings reincarnate into the lower animal, vegetable, or mineral kingdoms, and below, due to a person's negative actions. Would you please share with us your knowledge about this topic?

TJL All entities in those "so called" lower than human kingdoms are equipped with a soul specific to that kingdom that allows them to progress in their own manner towards entering our human kingdom. After the human level has been reached the soul is unique and its complexity prevents a back slide into a so called lower realm through the process of reincarnation. There is no cosmic punishment involved in the law of Karma. It simply relates to an effect that your action has set in motion. After a soul is born into a human body it continues its evolution within the human kingdom until enlightenment is achieved.

An action completely separate from reincarnation is called "annihilation" and takes place when a soul fails to advance in any way such as an individual that takes part in mass murder. That entities primordial matter is recycled to start again at the lowest aspect of life on earth.

QUESTION 41

Q How did humanity become so lost regarding the concept of reincarnation and our immortal souls?

TJL In ancient Earth cycles, the concept of our souls making us essentially immortal was a well-known concept. Over the mists of time many other concepts and opposing thoughts were introduced by major religions to teach several variations of that truth. Wise avatars incarnated to teach us ethical behavior and the advancement and unfoldment of our highest consciousness which is preserved in the soul. Their teachings reflected successfully advancing our soul through reincarnation adhering to the cosmic Law of Cause and Effect. Much confusion now exists within the Christian Church through their current doctrine that each soul only exists one lifetime and then is sent to heaven or hell. I am certain Jesus would be incredulous that the doctrine of reincarnation that he taught and which was carried on for 500 years after his passing, was removed from his teaching.

QUESTION 42

Q In our discussion about past lifetimes you mentioned that people eventually advance their souls to a level where they are able to access memories about their past lives. You also spoke about a process referred to as past life regression that anyone interested could access some of those memories. I have been told that you have an awareness about some of your past lives and I was wondering if there might be an experience that you would be willing to share this evening that has special significance to who you are this lifetime?

TJL The life I will share with you here tonight, I rarely speak about though I realize it had tremendous impact on who I am. The era was the late 12th century, ending in the early 13th century. It was a significant time on our planet because I believe we were close to creating the true peace on Earth that many of us on the planet still seek. I was a leader in a group known as the Cathars in Southern France during those years. It was a time when the legend of the Holy Grail was spreading over the entire continent. Our doctrine was essentially Gnostic in origin. We believed in reincarnation as well as equality for all people, including women, who we held in high esteem and revered through the divine feminine principle. We spoke out against intercessors such as priests acting as necessary interpreters between man and God. As you might guess, this concept created quite a stir among the Roman Church hierarchy that we bitterly opposed. We scoffed at their bogus pardons, their cruelty to their opposition, and the obvious corruption of many that made up a greedy priesthood. We encouraged wisdom based on direct, personal, and mystical experience. We taught meditation and encouraged several aspects of it to connect with the Divine. We essentially saw existence in our material world as a struggle between the forces of Light and Dark. We viewed humanity as spiritual beings learning their life lessons in a material realm. The Church at that time was based on the male principle of material wealth and power so we became a major threat to their dominance and dogma. We preached about love. It was our opinion based on our research that a more accurate account of the life of Jesus was that he was an advanced being who had lived many lifetimes before the one he is known as "Jesus the Christ." He was a great teacher, and an avatar that lived long after his reported demise on the cross. We felt that every human being was a son or daughter of God. Our teachers were comprised of both men and women. So possessive was the Roman Church at that time of their power over humanity that any lay person caught reading the Bible was promptly executed. Please check your history books to verify all of this.

Our ideas were beginning to spread like wild-fire throughout Europe before Pope Innocent the Third, began a direct extermination of most of us. Our culture which embraced certain basic Christian, Gnostic, Jewish, and Muslim ideas with equal enthusiasm disappeared off the face of our planet.

QUESTION 43

Q Why is it so important to be humble on the "Sacred Way" you walk?

TJL Only in humility can a human being's sacred powers be both utilized and enhanced. A selfish person will never reach the heights I have spoken about here. The true name for a shaman in Grandfather's lineage was *icshe wichasa,* "humble being." It is extremely important we act as humble shamans to provide our service in the manner it was meant to be carried out with kindness and caring. I recommend you avoid those who I refer to as sorcerers, who utilize lower aspects of this knowledge for selfish reasons. They are usually boastful and charge exorbitant fees for their services and may unintentionally or intentionally do you harm.

QUESTION 44

Q Could you explain to me why Buddhists do not believe in God, or a Great Spirit as you define it?

TJL It is not that Buddhists rule out God completely as a supreme being within our reality. It is that they state that there is no immutable proof that God exists. They believe that our concept of God is an acquired notion.

QUESTION 45

Q What led you to the decision to write about your experiences in your "Sacred Earth" books?

TJL I was asked to do so by my spirit guide. My first book, "In the Spirit of Black Elk: Preserving a Sacred Way" took me approximately 8 years to complete. I am a very private person and quite frankly was hesitant at first to proceed. Before Grandfather passed away I explained what I was doing and his encouragement sealed the deal. My initial response was to preserve for future generations what I learned from those who taught me, whose deep connection to the Earth was profound. It was my feeling that the highest aspects of this ancient wisdom have never been clearly understood by most people. This "Sacred Way" goes well beyond working with some of the lower earth spirits that exist as has been reported by many. I felt I had a unique opportunity and a great responsibility to add to the known archival information on record and at the same time honor my mentors' lives as extraordinary and interesting. I view "An Angel and a Shaman" as another level of this wisdom in which I share stories about my experiences and further details about this unique walk I have been on. It took me only one year to write my second book.

QUESTION 46

Q Love appears to be a central theme throughout your writing and teaching. Would you agree with this assessment?

TJL Yes, I have a clear understanding that it is one of the greatest gifts mankind can experience. I have mentioned often in my own teaching that "Love your neighbor as yourself" may be the most profound statement ever made regarding how to work within the Great Law of Cause and Effect successfully while we occupy our bodies on Earth.

QUESTION 47

Q What figure out of Lakota history do you most admire?

TJL Stories several elders shared with me about Crazy Horse have left a lasting impression upon me. He referred to what we call God as "Everything Everywhere Spirit." He understood clearly that we live in a world shaped by Spirit. He knew every tree, every stone, every river, all things have a Spirit form. Those he called *taku skan*, "the world of the intelligence of being." He shared that this world embraced imagination, soul, and fertility. He called it sacred and the essence of reality. He never surrendered during his lifetime. He never signed away any land or rights of his people. No photograph, painting, or sketch exists of him. He was an intriguing example of a truly free human being. Sadly with the oncoming landslide of the European invasion of his world, he met his demise at their hands.

QUESTION 48

Q You have advised us, whenever possible, to examine each situation we face in life from all directions just as your Grandfather advised you. Could you shed further light on this statement?

TJL Most people when faced with a difficult situation or problem make their decision about it from a single point of view in a spur of the moment fashion. What Grandfather taught me was to view that same problem from each cardinal direction, as well as above and below, as if viewing it from a clear sphere simultaneously. These powers of the directions were sometimes referred to as the powers of the four winds.

Over my 28 years of working in this manner I came to envision a helping angel in each of those directions and received tremendous help on many occasions from those very powerful sources.

QUESTION 49

Q What is your take on the mythical Akashic Records?

TJL The Akashic Records are a body of knowledge that contains everything that every soul has ever thought, said, or done over the course of its existence as well as its future possibilities. In the process of opening these records a person must transition from a state of ordinary consciousness to a state of universal consciousness in which you recognize your absolute oneness with Great Spirit.

This state allows you to perceive the impressions and vibrations at a manageable rate which allows you to integrate them into your human experience. Akasha is a Sanskrit word describing the primary substance out of which all things are formed. It is comprised of such fineness that even the slightest vibration affects it. This energy can be described as a quality of light that our thoughts and emotions register upon. Therefore the records hold the archive of each soul as it has existed from lifetime to lifetime as different human beings. They are the catalogue of our experiences as an individual as we grow into our divine nature.

QUESTION 50

Q How do you respond to those who believe that physical life is all there is and that when we die there is nothing more?

TJL When I hear this type of statement I realize that the person making it is taking their beginning steps on their own pathway of attainment. We all must start somewhere and I usually point out to these people that eventually they will reach a place of development where they too will recognize that the fuller life of the soul is what is paramount as we live our lives from lifetime to lifetime on Earth. The soul eventually discovers the consciousness that we do not die in the sense of those who believe we live only one physical life, and death is our singular end. The advanced soul realizes that when we leave our material bodies behind, we will eventually occupy a new body each lifetime, until the perfection of our soul is realized. The advanced soul sees physical life for what it really is and understands the highest aspects of being human help us with the unfoldment of soul.

QUESTION 51

Q What is your reaction to those who live for their luxurious toys and bask in the superficial pleasures of life only paying attention only to their selfish desires?

TJL It is quite hazardous to ignore your soul and become a slave to your physical things. I have seen Karma remove those physical objects from a person who should know better and the Law of Cause and Effect will eventually teach this type of individual that true happiness can only be acquired from an inner pathway. Enjoy the normal pleasures of life in moderation but always retain your mastery over them. As a person advances spiritually they are apt to lead a simple life with great joy.

QUESTION 52

Q Will you clarify further for us your words within our ceremony tonight that we are each eternal beings?

TJL The life you are experiencing now is a minute fragment of your "Great Life" that extends lifetime after lifetime, new body after new body, each adding a significant piece to the higher self that you preserve within your soul.

QUESTION 53

Q Would you help me understand more clearly your reference to the word "powers" as it relates to your "Sacred Way?"

TJL The powers gained as a person advances along any sacred pathway of attainment are what my Grandfather referred to as supernatural powers or spiritual talent. They are acquired over the course of many years of helping others, sometimes many lifetimes. What most people do not understand is that they can only be applied to unselfish purposes.

Those who seek and gain worldly power at the expense of others never receive these special gifts. As I have suggested to you, your spiritual talent will automatically grow and mature as you move forward with the unfoldment of your soul each lifetime. Worldly power will be left behind as you discard each body that you temporarily occupy.

QUESTION 54

Q In your first book your angel speaks to you about "the sacred peace" you will gain when you discover the place in the northern lands she sees for you and your family. What can you share with us here tonight about that sacred peace that you found?

TJL The sacred peace of the awakened soul evolves over many lifetimes and eventually comes to those who are conscious of the real spiritual existence that I have shared with you in my writing, teaching, and art. That peace of a mature soul grows sweeter over the years and is usually part of a pathway influenced by the higher powers.

QUESTION 55

Q Would you be willing to share any other details with us tonight about the process that you went through to find the place your angel described to you during your initiation within the Great Pyramid?

TJL We initially moved to Central California so our children could reacquaint themselves with their Grandparents who they saw only on special occasions prior to our move. This also removed us from the danger that apparently existed in the San Diego area. From that temporary residence we explored possibilities from Northern California, Oregon, and Washington. On a camping trip to the Pacific Northwest my spiritual guides directed us to the fishing village and artist community we eventually settled in. The weather was glorious at about 85 degrees. The eagle nation came to visit us in great numbers along the way. The town was having a salmon festival and we all feasted on salmon and met so many nice people it felt quite obvious we were home. After renting a house for less than a year our property revealed itself to us and we have lived here happily for many years. Though many others have joined us on the point we settled upon, we still enjoy the island like quiet and privacy that we sought within the big trees, by the moving waters, and the clean air that my angel described to me within the Great Pyramid.

QUESTION 56

Q You spoke to us about the wealth a pure soul accumulates during his or her time on their pathway of attainment. Would you please clarify for us what you meant by this statement?

TJL The wealth I refer to is the knowledge and wisdom you will acquire as you mature and advance on your journey of the soul.

QUESTION 57

Q Why should I believe anything you say is true?

TJL When your soul is ready for these truths you will instinctively understand that they are indeed true at which point your awakening will allow you to continue with your progress on the soul journey we are all taking together.

QUESTION 58

Q You seem to possess a wealth of knowledge and wisdom regarding the human soul. Why is that and could you give me any further information about that subject?

TJL It is knowledge I came into to this lifetime with which was further enhanced by my last 28 years of helping people as a humble shaman. I believe shamans are specialists regarding this subject matter and have been so since the first age of mankind perhaps due to the enlightened states we are able to manifest. You will grow into your spiritual consciousness as you progress on your own sacred path during this lifetime and those that will follow. When you reach a certain maturity within that evolving spiritual consciousness there comes a dawning of perception regarding the certainty that really who you are, "is a soul." Most religions do not ever explain that fact clearly. The "I" that is you does not die.

QUESTION 59

Q You explained in your writing quite beautifully the initial contact with your angel that you experienced within the King's Chamber of the Great Pyramid in Egypt. Could you share any other details about this event and how the dialogue you have shared with her over the years comes about?

TJL Out of the silence usually before, during, or after a ceremony her voice entered my field of consciousness to help someone in some manner. Sometimes the person being helped was contacted directly by her and they also heard her voice speaking to them. During my initiation in the Great Pyramid she appeared in a physical form that was transparent yet had substance as I described in my first book. She explains she comes from a plane of consciousness different from our own, and that the song she gave me was intended to help me dial in to her frequency to hear her words more clearly throughout our years of working together. It also solidified my knowing that we had physically met within that sacred temple.

QUESTION 60

Q What else can you share with us about our planet?

TJL We have been here many lifetimes upon the present incarnation of our Earth. We have also experienced other planetary systems and worlds. Some of those were destroyed before our solar system was formed. Our planet was formed as the result of the evolution of other planets and some of you inhabited some of those older worlds.

QUESTION 61

Q Would you please comment on the power of thoughts?

TJL Thoughts are literally things. They are extremely powerful and can remain in existence long after you have a memory of sending them. An appropriate analogy would be when flowers with a specific scent have occupied a space in your home and then they are removed. You are usually still able to smell their scent in the air long after their physical presence has vanished. So too, are thoughts able to carry power.

QUESTION 62

Q I would like to ask you a question that arose for me after reading "an Angel and a Shaman" in which an Aboriginal elder explained to you that telepathy was their primary means of communication with each other. Could you share anything further about telepathy between humans?

TJL Among human beings, it is the communication of one mind with another. Sight, hearing, smell, taste, and touch are part of our physical and astral bodies and a sixth sense also exists that can be cultivated in which we become aware of the thoughts emanating from the minds of others, even those at great distances away.

Therefore, telepathy is the receiving by a person consciously or unconsciously of vibrations or thought forms sent consciously or unconsciously from one mind to another. Because thought vibrations penetrate the matter that our physical bodies are made of, no outward openings are necessary for its use.

QUESTION 63

Q You spoke about the pineal gland in our ceremony this evening, could you explain what it is and how it functions?

TJL It is found in the brain of every human being, near the middle of our skulls, almost directly above the top of our spinal columns. It is reddish gray, cone shaped, and resides in front of the cerebellum. This is the organ through which the brain receives impressions by the medium of vibrations caused by thoughts from other human brains. It is what makes the telepathy dialogue possible.

QUESTION 64

Q I have been interested in the works of Carlos Castaneda for many years. In his last book "The Active Side of Infinity" he speaks about a frightening group of entities that Don Juan's lineage was aware of in Mexico that he called "mud shadows." In "An Angel and a Shaman" you speak about your sacred pipe work that included transmuting potentially dark energies left in those environments from a past age. Have you read this Castaneda book and did you ever run across those entities or anything similar?

TJL I read most of Castaneda's work about thirty years ago and for some reason only discovered the last book he ever wrote by the title you mentioned at a used book store several months ago. I found the chapter he devoted to the entities you mention quite interesting. The Light work I spoke about in "An Angel and a Shaman" did indeed include transmuting dark energies of an unknown origin left in that environment from an ancient time. Because of the intensity of the dark forces that I encountered I explained in that writing at times I had doubts during those years that I held the powers necessary to survive the onslaught of whatever it was I was up against. By Castaneda's description his "mud shadows" had the ability to inflict damage upon human beings and he felt incredibly fearful and disorientated after his own encounter. He died not long after that event and I wondered based on my own experiences if it was not directly related. Don Juan stated to Castaneda that his lineage of sorcerer's, not to be confused with shaman's, had no answer for the terror and darkness of what he referred to as the "mud shadows." The sacred pipe ceremonies my angel directed me to accomplish were designed to heal the environments I was working in. As I explained after one encounter I returned home extremely ill and am certain some dark force had stalked me as a result of my efforts. On another occasion my good friend Michael who had been a consultant on our seaquarium team joined me in a ceremony. He would also attest to the fact that we were nearly overcome by what may have been exactly what Castaneda ran into. While completing my ceremony on a beach near where our work had taken us, I began to feel uneasy for no particular reason. As I looked at a patch of water no more than 20 yards from where we sat the previously calm waters began to boil with fish, meaning they were jumping out of the water in a frenzied action that began to hold my complete attention. A shadow soon appeared to envelope us, and it became darker than normal only in our specific area. I was left with an overwhelming feeling of fear and dread, and if I had not been properly trained by my Angel my inclination would have been to get up and run. On that occasion I called in the white light that I have utilized for protection on other occasions and the shadow receded and disappeared entirely. Michael also felt what I was feeling, and seemed to have been affected adversely by the entire experience for some time afterwards. He made reservations to return home the next day and boarded a plane never to return to our project. We remain close friends and on the rare occasion that we speak about those moments we usually express how fortunate we are to have survived. And so it was, and continues to be a part of the Great Mystery of that chapter of my life.

QUESTION 65

Q When you completed your stone-people-lodge ceremony with the physicists and others described in your second book, clairvoyance was brought into the scientific conversation. Could you speak further about clairvoyant phenomena?

TJL I believe clairvoyance is possible because of a person's access to the astral plane. As I explained to you this evening, each of our physical senses exist on the astral plane in a corresponding manner. Therefore, while a person inhabits the astral plane, astral sight enables them to receive astral light vibrations made up of more subtle rays of light than ordinary rays of light in our physical realm. This allows them to see scenes we are not able to see. Some people with this skill are able to view impressions from great distances, while others are capable of utilizing this skill only in locations nearby.

QUESTION 66

Q Could you explain what clairaudience is from your perspective?

TJL Clairaudience is the gift of hearing by a person consciously or unconsciously the vibrations of a voice sent consciously or unconsciously from one being to another. The actual voice is heard in this circumstance rather than a telepathic communication that has registered directly in your mind.

QUESTION 67

Q After reading your books it appears that several Grandfathers and Grandmothers became a part of your life to become special teachers in one way or another. Is there another elder along those lines that we have perhaps not heard about who influenced your walk in any way?

TJL Your question is especially interesting to me because I only knew one of my Grandfathers this lifetime, via bloodline, due to my Dad's father's untimely death before I was born. It has quite frankly fascinated me that so many elders have been a part of my path. Yes, there is another Grandfather that Carol and I adopted while we lived in backcountry San Diego. He was a professor of mine during my years of working on my Masters Degree in Painting and Drawing at SDSU, Thomas Tibbs. At the time we met he had been recently retired as the Director of the La Jolla Museum of Contemporary Art. He had visited the studios and discussed art with many of the prominent abstract expressionist artists of our age, during his New York years of the 1950's. As you may or may not know that era is considered perhaps the most prominent in the history of a truly American art with the likes of Rothko, Pollack, DeKooning, and many others. His stories undoubtedly inspired me over the many years of our friendship and abstract expressionism has always been one of my own primary themes throughout my years of making art. As his health began to decline, after his wife's passing, he moved to the Pacific Northwest to spend several quality years near our family before his own passing.

QUESTION 68

Q Would you care to comment on the term human magnetism?

TJL That term refers to the universal energy I describe as prana. Prana is acquired naturally through your breathing, your food, and the fluids you take into your body. To maximize the prana you take in you must form an image of the energy entering specific areas of your body where you are aware it is needed. Do not let the simplicity of this description cause you to under-estimate its value as without prana your physical body will not survive.

QUESTION 69

Q What other advice do you have for us regarding our bodies or "robes" as you describe them?

TJL Our bodies are the temples where Spirit resides, so tend them well, do not abuse them, and create a worthy instrument to walk on this Earth.

QUESTION 70

Q Would you care to comment on the healing touch concept utilized by many in the medical field at this time, whereby hands move over the body generally a few inches above areas that need attention directing healing energies to an affected part.

TJL I believe advanced workers of this technique are often effective in helping their patients. Though they might not understand why it works, what they are actually doing is directing an increased supply of prana to an organ or affected part. Sometimes positive thoughts are added to the healing equation also fully charged with pranic life force helping a patient rebuild and repair his body to normal function. Other times the aura of the healer involved can bring immediate healing to an ailment if it is radiating a proper spectrum of color.

QUESTION 71

Q You mentioned "unity consciousness" in our stone-people-lodge this evening and I am still unclear what exactly you meant. Could you explain what it is and how it fits into your "Sacred Way."

TJL My angel explained to me that "unity consciousness" was established on our planet several hundred thousand years ago by the "Great Light Brother and Sisterhood." Jesus attempted to teach this concept to his followers when he stated that if two or more human beings are gathered together they have the ability to create with their thoughts and intentions. Jesus knew that within this group context tremendous power existed, which is why it is also referred to as "Christ Consciousness." This concept became the foundation for the prayer circles of the Christian Church and obviously fits into the prayer circle within a stone-people-lodge.

QUESTION 72

Q Of what use are my experiences gained in a former life if I do not remember them in the body I rebirth into?

TJL Your experiences are not completely lost to you since the highest of those become a part of the fifth, sixth, and seventh principles of your soul which I have explained to you in my seven principles of being human teaching. Eventually you will reach a state of advancement where you will have the opportunity to remember past lives important to you souls unfoldment but until then know that all of those experiences will create the "I" that is you as your soul matures. Eventually my angel states that all human beings will attain enlightenment within the seventh world on the seventh incarnation of planet Earth and again become one with Great Spirit.

QUESTION 73

Q You mentioned "table tapping" before our ceremony tonight as one of the many unusual serendipitous episodes in your life. What is it and would you be willing to tell us that story?

TJL During the time when I was leading stone-people-lodges in the back country of San Diego, California, a group of my friends asked me to join them to attend a "table tapping" session carried out by a woman spoken of in one of Shirley McLane's books. I had no idea what exactly "table tapping" was about other than the woman was known to bring forward information that often lead to healing in the people she worked with through her communication with spirits. When I arrived late for her program there were several hundred people entering the auditorium where the event was to take place in downtown San Diego. As I entered the building, another individual helping with the program was asking those of us in line if anyone wanted to participate up on the stage with the host, and I for some reason was moved to volunteer immediately. I had unfortunately missed the dialogue that I was supposed to have some sickness that needed curing to participate. When my name was called as the first participant of the evening I sat at a fairly heavy oak table with two straight backed chairs, one of which was being utilized by the host. When she asked me what illness of mine needed attention I candidly let her know I felt in perfect health and wondered why she would ask such a thing. She was at first a bit flustered and slightly annoyed by my response but rebounded enough to explain to me the nature of my error being on stage. However, while sitting at her table slightly embarrassed, with our hands lightly touching its top surface, she began stating each letter of the alphabet after which upon certain letters the table would appear to rise on its own. She explained to the audience that someone from the great beyond wanted to contact me. When she got to N, the table went airborne. I took a quick look underneath and realized nothing was attached... then E...then L...then L again. At first it did not register with me who Nell was, and then I realized Nell was my dear Grandmother that I knew as my Grandma Lystra. Nell was her first name and she was always special to me. We had always been very close until her passing several years before. I was a bit shocked at first and then our host said that Nell had a message for me. We went through the alphabet scenario over the next several minutes and my Grandmother Nell made the table rise for each of the letters which spelled out, "I LOVE YOU GRANDSON, and I AM FINE," as if she had read my mind wondering about how she was. On the last letter the table nearly raised onto my lap. The rest of the evening our host addressed the needs of others who had specific problems, and I sat dazed with the knowledge that we had made contact with my favorite Grandmother. And so it was!

QUESTION 74

Q You have shared with us often how important it is to be in service to humanity. What do you consider our greatest duty within that service?

TJL Be kind whenever the opportunity arises and never abuse the powers you have acquired along your "Sacred Way."

QUESTION 75

Q Do you consider us to be true masters over our own destiny?

TJL Every thought, word, and action has an effect on your future, therefore, we are each masters of our own destiny via the Universal Law of Cause and Effect.

QUESTION 76

Q How is our rebirth into a new life determined and under what conditions does that occur?

TJL Your desires, aspirations, likes, and dislikes all play a part in that process along with the more prominent unfolding of Spirit within your soul. What is determined by the higher powers is directly related to your soul's future advancement rather than the comfort you might enjoy in a life in which you had not much to gain.

QUESTION 77

Q The "Sacred Way" you have shared with us tonight is profound and extremely appealing to me.
Is there another sacred pathway of attainment
from a past life that you feel may have influenced
your direction this lifetime?

TJL "The Way of the Tao" I practiced and respected very deeply in a past existence. It is Chinese
in origin, and literally translated as "the way of
nature" in which all things come into being out of
Darkness into Light, then pass out of Light back

into Darkness, back and forth throughout time. Light and Dark were considered identical, only separated by our human minds. Neither principle is thought to be better than the other. Neither principle is thought to be stronger than the other. The secret of the Tao then is to understand no matter what comes your way it is neither good nor bad, it simply is part of your way.

QUESTION 78

Q Do you believe in what many call the devil?

TJL No I do not. That term actually became a part of human consciousness when modern church hierarchies began to equate evil with darkness, thereby combining those two words into devil. The word began to be used often after the Zoroastrian belief which saw evil in the Hindu devas or nature spirits who became devils in their teaching from that point forward.

QUESTION 79

Q The work I have chosen to be in service to the universe with is Hospice, the end of life care for those ready to leave there bodies. What would be the most enlightened view I could share with those who might be ready to hear your view of this time of transition?

TJL You can share with them that which we call death should be likened to falling asleep and waking up next morning. Let them know that death will seem as but a temporary loss of consciousness.

You can tell them that life is continuous and that the object of life is the development, growth, and unfoldment of the soul. Let them know that the soul works as well out of body as well as in it. Let them know that eventually an entirely new and different kind of body will be required.

QUESTION 80

Q How old are our souls?

TJL Our souls are ancient beyond your imagination. They have progressed and developed in many ways, always moving higher on our spiral pathways over many lifetimes. There are countless worlds and planes that we will eventually experience until the seventh world of the seventh renewal of planet Earth at which time we will all reach perfect

enlightenment. The Buddha referred to this re-
connection with Great Spirit as nirvana.

QUESTION 81

Q Why do so many human beings seem to be sleep walking through their lives in an unconscious manner?

TJL The majority of human beings have not reached the stage in the spiritual growth of their souls to be totally conscious. Yet many like you have the potential to awaken to the truth about Great Spirit this lifetime.

QUESTION 82

Q Where does mankind stand within the hierarchy of kingdoms on this world and others?

TJL There are many forms of life lower than human beings, and many forms of life higher than human beings. Some of those beings are so far advanced above our present plane of development that we are not able to even imagine them.

QUESTION 83

Q If reincarnation is such an obvious fact of life, why do I not carry any recollection of my past lives?

TJL Your soul will eventually advance in its growth and unfoldment to recognize those lifetimes that are important for you to remember. You will discover the truth then and never be the same after this awakening.

QUESTION 84

Q I am aware that you are an ardent believer in education and knowledge acquisition, and that you have studied the words of many of the world's great masters and teachings. I am a Buddhist and wonder what your perspective might be of the man we refer to as Guatama Buddha?

TJL Buddha's personal evolution is fascinating to me. His stance on non-violence was truly inspirational. His teachings on the importance of simplicity within this material world have had a profound effect on me. His altruism mirrors that of a humble shaman. The pragmatism of his ethics may be his greatest contribution to mankind. He taught about suffering, understanding the origin of suffering, understanding the extinction of suffering, and utilizing that wisdom to reach nirvana and complete union with Great Spirit which he called non-being. He taught we must free our thoughts from lust, ill will, and cruelty. He taught we must abstain from lying, encourage concord, and avoid harsh language. He taught we must abstain from killing, stealing, or unlawful sexual intercourse. He taught we should choose a livelihood that does no harm to another being. He taught we should avoid evil, overcome it if faced with it, and be good to all beings. He taught we should be attentive, and be able to concentrate when necessary. He believed the culmination of these efforts would lead to enlightenment and I believe Buddhism is certainly one of the pathways of attainment in which to get there.

QUESTION 85

Q Could you please clarify for me what an avatar is?

TJL Yes, you have heard me refer to the great beings that have walked on planet Earth such as Jesus the Christ, as avatars. These beings are special incarnations that surrender themselves to pure consciousness and truth and in so doing merge their individual consciousness with the universal consciousness. It is said that they choose to come to our world during a particular Earth cycle to help raise the vibration of humanity during that world age.

QUESTION 86

Q Would you mind clarifying in as much detail as time allows us tonight what your guides have informed you to be true about what happens after the physical death of a human being?

TJL When the death of a human being takes place the force which holds our cells together is withdrawn and our physical bodies disintegrate. The soul leaves the body it occupied during that lifetime. The influence of your higher mind is withdrawn. Your astral body rises from your physical body like a cloud of thin luminous vapor. As the cord that connects the two becomes thinner it eventually breaks. This event is sometimes visible to those still living. Eventually this astral body is discarded and it disintegrates. Your whole life from infancy to old age passes before your mental vision. Many events are made clear as picture after picture passes before the departing soul. Often times a whole life is better understood. A semi-conscious blissful state then sets in and the lower or instinctive mind dissolves. Each soul awakens when only the highest aspects of the intellect and spiritual mind remain. Your soul then passes to the plane within the astral world suitable to its progress and development. Preparation eventually begins there for your next incarnation. Souls that reach the higher planes often spend more time out of body between lives. After a soul attains a certain level of consciousness past lives are revealed and more choices occur. There are numerous planes of disembodied existence. The highest of those cannot be described while in a material body, however, they are often confused with what some call heaven. The lowest astral planes are very similar to Earth life without the limitations.

QUESTION 87

Q I have had some medicine men tell me that I should never share my visions with others. Would you care to comment on that perspective?

TJL I believe visons come for many reasons and that each one should be examined from all directions. If it involves information only for you then honor that information. However, it may also include information for the good of many and that form of vision should be shared with a giving heart.

QUESTION 88

Q You explained in your first two books how you were given the name Red Hawk, by Spirit, in a naming ceremony with your Grandfather. Did you ever consider utilizing the name Red Hawk as the author of that material?

TJL I considered using my Spirit given name Red Hawk, however, I ended up choosing to utilize my full name of Torrey James Lystra to honor my Father whose first name was James. He was a star athlete in four sports throughout his high school years and intended to play college baseball and football before the breakout of WWII, and the untimely death of his father. My childhood years were idyllic in the farm country of the Central Valley of California. I remember fondly "many catches" in our backyard together, baseball hitting lessons, learning to swim in the irrigation canals while mostly riding on his back against those dangerous currents, and boxing lessons in our garage where we strapped on our gloves and head protection and I was taught how to defend myself. Later in life our walks and talks while playing golf were filled with laughter, joy, and always competitive. On the day my five member High School golf team and I set a record for low scoring for a championship level California golf course, I discovered him hiding behind a tree on the back nine so as "not to add any undue pressure to my outing." I knew him to be a kind man whose physical prowess and toughness were respected by all who knew him. He told me he felt lucky to have survived "WorldWar II" in which he served as a paratrooper. He explained his assignment to his unit's baseball, football, boxing, and swim teams had more than likely kept him alive. On one of these "safe deployments" he once fought the seventh ranked middleweight boxer of the world and lived to tell the tale. After the war he became a Post man. It was a job he enjoyed because he loved to walk in nature and loved people, a path I also followed, though I became a park ranger. He retired many years later at the age of 55, but suffered greatly with the rest of our family during my mother's 12 year battle with Alzheimer's disease. His final words on Earth spoken to me were, "I did the best that I could," a humble sentiment that I admire deeply. Though "Red Hawk" answered many of these questions while in "the enlightened state of a shaman," I wrote those books and recapitulated these questions and answers as Torrey James Lystra, in a manner most conducive to your understanding.

Mi tak u ye oyasin.
    To all my relations